HOUSTON HEIGHTS
1891-1991

A Historical Portrait
and
Contemporary Perspective

Text by G. Randle Pace and Deborah Markey

TRIBUNE PUBLISHING COMPANY
Houston, Texas

Cover Design: Thorp Studio
Printed in the U.S.A.
on 100# Lithofect Gloss Text by Brandt & Lawson Printing, Inc.
815 Live Oak Street, Houston, Texas 77003

Tribune Publishing Company
2150 W. 18th, Suite 213, Houston, Texas 77008

Centennial First Edition

"HOUSTON HEIGHTS 1891-1991, A Historical Portrait and Contemporary Perspective" centennial photography book has been underwritten by the following patrons and the Houston Heights Association is grateful to them. Proceeds from the sale of this book will benefit various community projects of the Houston Heights Association.

GOLD SPONSORS:

Earl & Martha Austin
North Houston Pole Line Corp.

SILVER SPONORS:

Exxon Chemical Americas

Houston Heights Tribune
In Memory of Milton & Nella Wiesenthal

James R. Moffett

BRONZE SPONSORS:

AMI Heights Hospital
BABB Houston Public Relations
Carter & Cooley Deli
Clayton Lee Plumbing
First Heights Bank, fsb
Dennis & Laura Virgadamo - Harmony Electric
Heights Business Women's Group
Heights Funeral Home
Kaplan's Ben-Hur
Lawrence Marshall Chevrolet
The Leader Newspapers
Merchants Bank
Texas Commerce Bank - Reagan
Elwaine Barrett - Union Motors

ACKNOWLEDGEMENTS

The Houston Heights Association wishes to acknowledge with sincere appreciation the following people who devoted countless hours and unselfish dedication toward the production of this book:

Gus Kopriva - Curator of Centennial Photography Exhibit;
Deborah Markey - Exhibit Chairman; Randy Pace - Project Historian;

Paul Babb of BABB Houston - text editing; Richard Carson of the Houston Chronicle - photographic reproductions; Sharon Lauder of Houston Heights Tribune - securing financial sponsors; Terry Burge and Tracy Vessels of The Leader Newspapers - photographs and newsfiles; Nancy Kienholz - book design and layout; Charlie Thorp of Thorp Studio - cover design; Amy Woodrick of Tribune Publishing - layout and typesetting.

In addition the Houston Heights Association would like to thank the following individuals for their contributions:

Jenny Bennett, Centennial Co-Chairman and Bart Truxillo, President of the Houston Heights Association and Centennial Co-Chairman; Sims McCutcheon, Librarian, Houston Public Library; Mary Culbertson, Librarian, University of Houston School of Architecture; Steve Baron and Mildred Dupuis - historical photograph identification. Special thanks for project support from John Blass, Donna Carson, Sharon Kopriva, Richard Markey and Neil Sackheim. The Houston Heights Association would also like to thank those individuals who loaned their photographs for inclusion in this photographic history book.

Special appreciation is extended to the staff of the Houston Metropolitan Research Center (HMRC), a division of the Houston Public Library. HMRC contains a wide range of sources detailing the development and growth of Houston and its surrounding areas. HMRC houses the largest existing photographic collection of Houston, consisting of approximately 500,000 prints and negatives. Special thanks to Chuck Hamilton, HMRC Photographer; Archivists, Nancy Hadley, Dr. Tom Krenek, Louis Marchiafava; Texas Room Librarians, Ann Douglas, Doris Glasser, Ellen Hanlon, Will Howard and Douglas Weiskopf.

The Houston Heights Association is deeply indebted to the following professional photographers, who, being Heights residents, were asked to provide a "contemporary perspective" to the centennial photography exhibit. Their works, as a result, depict all aspects of our special neighborhood. Except where noted as private collections (*), all photographers have graciously donated their work to the Heights Museum Collection.

Todd August	John Everett
Gary Bankhead	Tom Fox
Bruce Bennett	Bill Frazier
Dixon Bennett	Frank Golden
Suzanne Bloom*	Paul Hester
Donna Carson	Paul Howell
Richard Carson	C. Bryan Jones
George Craig	George Krause
Jeff DeBevec*	Frank Martin*
Robert Derr	Janice Rubin*
Dave Einsel	Tracy Vessels

HOUSTON HEIGHTS

The decade of the 1890s was an exciting period of development for Americans. Towns were becoming cities; cities were expanding. This was especially true in Texas, where speculators were drawn from other states. The Houston area attracted thousands of these adventurers, and it was in this climate that Houston Heights began. As early as 1886, Oscar Martin Carter, a self-made millionaire who had business interests in Nebraska and Colorado, brought to Houston a utopian vision for the approaching twentieth century. Carter's dream was to build a new type of town, a planned community where successful entrepreneurs and working people alike could live and work, in health and safety, as neighbors. Compared to Houston, a city plagued by yellow fever and devastating annual floods, Carter chose the ideal spot for his new community. Houston Heights, with an elevation 23 feet higher than downtown Houston, a natural sandy soil, rich vegetation, mature trees and artesian water sources, promised a sanctuary of health and well-being.

The land O.M. Carter and his Omaha and South Texas Land Company developed had long been an important area to the city of Houston. This section of southeastern Texas was first inhabited by Indians of the Coastal Plains. Although a Spaniard had visited the area in the early 16th century, it was not until 1745 that the French from New Orleans and the Spanish began to vie for control of the region. At that time, the area that included much of Houston Heights was controlled by Chief Canos of the Orcoquisacs. Chief Canos successfully played the two European powers against one another for many years.

In the early 19th century, as Americans began to settle in the region, grants of land were given to many of the pioneers by the Mexican government. The tracts of land awarded to John Richardson Harris and John P. Austin would eventually become the City of Houston, after Texas won independence as a Republic. Harris established a thriving port on Buffalo Bayou by the time the war began, and the town of Harrisburg grew around it. Harrisburg burned immediately before the Battle of San Jacinto in 1836, but was rebuilt after the war. Shortly after the Revolution, the town of Houston was laid out on the bayou above Harrisburg, and began its period of steady growth. Speculation began when the Allen Brothers, John and Augustus, acquired most of the Austin League and promoted this town in the wilderness, named after Sam Houston. Houston served as the capital of the Republic until 1839. During this period, when provisions were scarce and expensive, and housing was an even greater problem, a series of yellow fever epidemics inflicted the area. With each new outbreak of the disease, anxious residents sought to escape to the high area north of the White Oak Bayou. Soon a community of tents appeared on the opposite side of the bayou from Houston in the region that would later become Houston Heights.

The importance of Houston as a trading center grew rapidly as Americans increasingly moved westward. Houston's population swelled dramatically after the Civil War with a great influx of blacks from the South. The lack of adequate housing again aggravated a major bout with yellow fever in 1867. The period from 1874 to 1890 brought tremendous commercial expansion to Houston. Houston was the only major city, other than Galveston, that had access to the sea — but that access, by bayou waterways, was not fully developed. As such, it was the completion of the Aransas Pass Railway line to Houston in 1887, that marked the beginning of Houston's major growth. Next came 14 other railroad lines and even more reason to make Houston an inland port by making Buffalo Bayou more navigable.

O.M. Carter had convinced his eastern investors that Houston was destined for growth and the ideal place to invest heavily. Not only did Carter realize that Houston would attract major industries and thus experience population growth due to the jobs created by those industries, but he planned for many of the industries to locate in his planned development. He also knew that there would be a great need for housing and he wanted his development to provide the opportunity for home ownership.

Carter's vision included a transportation system that would bring passengers four miles from Houston to his planned community, a considerable distance in those days. However, in 1890, when most cities the size of Houston already had electric streetcar lines, Houston only had two mule-drawn systems. He arranged for the purchase and electrification of both systems, thus guaranteeing electric streetcars to Houston Heights. His investment gave potential investors the confidence to believe in his dream and invest in his totally planned community. It was also a very profitable venture, since the city was destined for tremendous growth as well.

By 1891, Carter attracted a corps of investors who set up the Omaha and South Texas Land Company. He even convinced some of them to give not just their money, but to live their lives in his utopian city. Carter recognized the desire of the growing middle class to move away from the noise and dirt of the crowded city. The company purchased 1,756 acres of land, and made over $500,000 worth of improvements, including utilities, streets and alleys, as well as parks and schools. The blocks were carefully arranged, some principal streets were covered with shell, and a waterworks system was established. Scattered open spaces supplemented the 60 foot-wide esplanade on Heights Boulevard. The trees and other natural features that now line the streets were planted during that early period of development. Carter also built a commercial strip at 19th and Ashland Streets and arranged for stores to open there to serve new residents. As was common in most promotional towns, he built a grand hotel (destroyed by fire, 1915) where prospective buyers could stay when they inspected the area.

The founding fathers also built a series of grand Victorian homes along Heights Boulevard, a broad, tree-lined central thoroughfare patterned after Commonwealth Avenue in Boston. Major industrial and commercial concerns were also attracted to Houston Heights by Carter and his associates before the turn of the century, thus completing his plan to develop a totally planned community in which to live and work.

The first lots to be sold in the new town were bought in 1893 by Silas D. Wilkins, a carpenter for the Omaha and South Texas Land Company who had helped ready the area for residents. Shortly thereafter, he built a home at 1541 Ashland Street and later became the second postmaster of Houston Heights. The Panic of 1893 (a nationwide economic recession) delayed the sale of lots somewhat, but by the time of the U.S. Census of 1900, Houston Heights had a total population of 800.

The first residence to be built on Heights Boulevard was appropriately the home of one of the original group of investors, D.D. Cooley. This Houston Heights landmark was built in 1893 as an example of the type of house to be built on the Boulevard. Cooley had come to Houston with Carter in 1890 as the general manager in charge of development for the Omaha and South Texas Land Company. From the beginning, he was extremely interested in making education easily available to the children of residents. He helped establish the first schools, including one for black children, and the first elementary school was named after him. In addition to land, Cooley had financial interests in oil, rice and insurance. The entire Cooley family was active socially in the neighborhood, and Mrs. Cooley donated the land upon which the clubhouse for the Houston Heights Woman's Club was built in 1912.

John Milroy was perhaps the most influential in the actual sale of lots and the movement of residents into the area. After gaining experience in real estate in the northwest, Milroy moved to Houston in 1893 to join Carter and his company. He and his family first lived at 1602 Harvard Street, but in 1897 moved into the large, intricately detailed home at 1102 Heights Boulevard, which is listed as a Registered Texas Historical Landmark and is one of over 100 structures listed in the National Register of Historic Places. For 20 years, Milroy was the general agent of the Houston Heights Office of Carter's company, assuming the power of attorney to all lands owned by O.M. Carter in Texas in 1906. Of equal importance were his eight terms as mayor of the municipality of Houston Heights, beginning in 1899. His children were also very active in the community and his older daughter, Helen, was widely associated with philanthropic and charitable groups. Milroy, who had been so instrumental in the initial success of Houston Heights, lived for only a few months after its annexation by Houston in 1918.

After Houston Heights was incorporated as a "village," and established its own municipal government in 1896, the first mayor elected was William G. Love. He served from the incorporation as a village in 1896 until 1899. His greater service to the Heights, however, was as its legal advisor. He was also appointed District Attorney for Harris and Galveston counties in 1907, and was elected to that position in the next year, serving until 1910. The large, Queen Anne style house at 1505 Heights Boulevard, with its classical porch detailing, was the home of Mayor Love until his death in 1926.

Although he was mayor of Houston Heights for six years following Milroy, David Barker was primarily a real estate investor. During his administration in Houston Heights (1907-13), several major improvements were accomplished. Heights Boulevard and several other streets were paved, schools were constructed, and the first fire station was built. Census figures of 1910 show an increase of more than 6,000 people since 1900 . These improvements were funded through bonds made possible by a charter from the State of Texas in 1911 that granted the town of Houston Heights the emergency power to tax. Perhaps the most interesting issue during his term of office was the matter of saloons in Houston Heights. On September 25, 1912, the residents voted to abolish places to purchase and consume alcoholic beverages and this law is still in force today. After proving his ability to handle public funds, Barker was elected county commissioner in 1914. As such, he ordered construction of the first concrete roads to be built in Harris County. And from 1928 until 1936, he served as the Land and Tax Commissioner of Houston. His well-preserved house at 116 E. 16th Avenue is a lasting reminder of the man who contributed much to his immediate community and the entire city. He was also president of the Park Place Company (1924-42) that developed a large subdivision east of Houston.

The home of the fourth mayor of Houston Heights, R.F. Isbell, also survives at 639 Heights Boulevard. It is noteworthy in that it features a large, second-floor room designed specifically to accommodate public meetings. The last mayor of Houston Heights was James B. Marmion, who served from 1914 until annexation in 1918. During his administration, a new fire station, city hall and jail was dedicated at Yale and W. 12th Streets. It was during Marmion's administration that the citizens of Houston Heights acknowledged that they could no longer supply a proper tax revenue to provide for the education of their children. It seems that the principal issue leading to annexation was the fear of having an inadequate local school system. Therefore, the citizens voted for annexation by the City of Houston in 1918.

From the outset, Carter planned Houston Heights as a modest community. There were a few land dealers, such as William A. Wilson, who acted as investors and developers in the area. But, in general, Carter sought to prevent speculation. His advertisements and his methods of promotion do not appear to have been aimed at the very wealthy, but at the growing class of white-collar workers, young professionals, and the skilled craftsmen of the working class. His philosophy has been maintained in practice by the residents over the years, whether consciously or not. The social and economic make-up of the present day Houston Heights probably is quite similar to that of 1915. The early occupants of the large, fanciful homes along the Boulevard were often doctors, lawyers or real estate professionals.

New industries directly related to oil, gas and shipping developed at the turn of the century in Houston and the Gulf Coast. Carter planned a portion of Houston Heights to attract some of that industry. Cotton mills, textile factories and oil refineries cropped up in the area during the initial years of development. One factory, the Oriental Textile Mill, even developed an area of about four blocks near the plant as a "Factory Village," a clustering of small houses for the workers.

The greater portion of Houston Heights was residential, however, and as it grew, it was not uncommon for a new resident to use the skills of his trade to build a home for his own family in addition to those he built professionally. Smaller, more modest cottages were built by resident-carpenters and other members of the building trade.

Expansion in Houston Heights paralleled advances of business and industry in Houston. The new commercial opportunities provided more people the prosperity to own homes. The majority of the early residents of Houston Heights belonged to this new middle class, and most of the homes in the neighborhood are styles of buildings found in the popular publications of the era. The first occupants of such houses were often bookkeepers, drillers of oil wells, teachers or small-businessmen. It was extremely important for such people to be part of a community. The green, open spaces in which children could play, the schools, the churches and the social and civic clubs were all necessary elements. One of the most important was the Houston Heights Woman's Club. It was established in 1900 by the merger of several other, more specialized groups. The club built a small bungalow style clubhouse at 1846 Harvard Street in 1912, which still serves as the headquarters for the group today. The purposes of the club included social work and charity, as well as educational instruction and cultural events. In addition to the Woman's Club, there were several more exclusive groups in the area with which the residents, particularly women, could affiliate.

Education was a very high priority among the leaders of Houston Heights from the beginning. Two elementary schools were constructed by 1900 to serve the northern and eastern sections of the community, and a high school was built in 1904. A few additions were made to these schools while Houston Heights existed as a separate municipality, but major new construction did not occur until after annexation of the town by Houston. New schools were built in the 1920s and a library was constructed at 1302 Heights Boulevard. This facility still serves as a cultural center of the community much as it did in the 1920s.

The city of Houston grew tremendously following World War I, partly because of the deepening of the ship channel and expansion of the petroleum and chemical industries. A major result of the expansion was the extension of several major streets and highways and, in later years, the construction of new interstate highway systems. The road and transportation expansions in the 1940s gave urban residents greater mobility to move to the suburbs and abandon the older, established neighborhoods. As a result of the exodus to the suburbs, Houston Heights also began to decline. Most larger homes were transformed into multi-family apartments or were neglected and deteriorated and eventually demolished. By 1970, the perception of the Heights was that of poverty. The pattern of promotion, booming growth, uncertainty and decline that was experienced by Houston Heights is similar to what happened to most inner-city neighborhoods. More commercial and industrial interests began to creep into the area after World War II, due to lack of zoning laws.

In 1973, residents and business owners organized the Houston Heights Association to work together toward maintaining the quality of life desired and toward preserving the historic fiber of the community. This renewed vitality has been attracting new residents, many of whom are the children of those people who moved to the suburbs long ago. In contrast to 100 years ago, the majority of these young, new residents are not moving to Houston Heights to build new homes but to restore the historic homes built by others. They are part of the national trend to buy an old house with all its charm and architectural distinction and restore it. Young professionals are also seeking the convenience of close-in living — only a short distance from work, cultural centers and restaurants. Once again, Houston Heights is developing a firm sense of identity and comraderie not much different from that found in the community created by O.M. Carter many years ago.

HOUSTON HEIGHTS
1891-1991

A Historical Portrait ...

This photograph of the interior of the Houston City Street Railway Company power house on Commerce Street, was published in Street Railway Review in June 1892. The capacity of the motor was 540 horsepower and the combined electric power was 360,000 kilowatts, equal to 500 horsepower. The company had 47 cars in operation and over 40 miles of track which constituted 11 separate routes. All the cars ran upon a central belt in the center of the city so that every car passed all points of the city on every trip. The company had 225 employees. Shown (left to right) is Fred Mundes, superintendent, H.F. MacGregor, vice president and general manager, and C.A. McKinney, secretary. O.M. Carter, president (not shown) first visited Houston as early as 1886 and was so inspired by the "progressive city" that he returned in September 1890, with the financial backing of northern and western investors to buy the two mule-drawn streetcar lines. Although he was given three years by Houston City Council to accomplish the task, he electrified the streetcar system in less than two years at a cost of over $500,000. (Photograph courtesy of Houston Public Library, HMRC)

On May 5, 1891, O. M. Carter, President of the American Loan & Trust Company, instructed his agents to begin buying 1,765 acres of land four miles northwest of Houston. The land was owned by Mrs. Sarah Brashear who sold it to Carter's agents for $45 per acre. After purchasing the tract, Carter filed the charter for the Omaha and South Texas Land Company in April 1892, and disclosed his intention to construct and operate on the tract, "a first class residence and manufacturers locality..." On May 2, 1892, scarcely one year after the Omaha and South Texas Land Company acquired the land, 300 men began clearing the land for "The Boulevard," later known as Heights Boulevard, the grand entrance into their residential area. The men lived in tent camps on the property during construction. They also began clearing the land for a steam railroad to the planned industrial section where Carter had enticed major manufacturing concerns to locate. A story has been told of an incident in which G.B. Hengen, who was engineer in charge of construction, would have been killed by a large pine tree as it was cut down in August 1892, had it not been for D.D. Cooley, Supervisor of Development. Mr. Cooley upon seeing the tree fall, called out "Mr. Hengen come at once!" Knowing that Mr. Hengen would respond immediately, Mr. Cooley knew that if he had warned him any other way, Mr. Hengen would not have had time to get out of the way of the falling tree. (Photograph courtesy of Carter & Cooley Deli)

Car No. 49 of the Houston City Street Railway Company, shown here outside the car barn on Commerce Street, was decorated for a parade in downtown Houston given in December, 1893 for prospective out-of-town investors. The parade consisted of several streetcars decorated with green boughs and alternating white and red incandescent lights. At the front of the first car was a five-pointed star six feet across, also made of incandescent lights. Between two decorated cars was an old mule-drawn streetcar, with the mule supplying the power. Each side was decorated with a sign saying "past". The second decorated car pulled an old mule-drawn car and from the inside, a small grey mule peeped out. On the sides of the mule-drawn car, a placard proclaimed, "I want a job." The first paid excursion on the streetcars to Houston Heights was taken by Car No. 2 on Sunday, October 23, 1892, at a cost of five cents. Every Sunday hence, streetcars took visitors to Houston Heights to view the wonders of the development. No matter how many cars were added to the trip, there never were enough cars to accommodate the curious visitors. On April 2, 1893, trailers were added to the cars for the first time, but even then, people rode out to Houston Heights on the tops of the streetcars. (Photograph courtesy of Houston Public Library, HMRC)

The Houston Heights Hotel on 19th Avenue had 50 rooms and was described in promotional literature as "...while not strictly in accord with any special class of architecture, it is charming in its quaint combination of gables, and invitingly attractive with its broad 22 foot galleries, giving it a semi-tropical appearance." The entire ground floor of the west wing was designated as a dance hall where many elegant affairs were held. On Sundays, it was also used by the St. Stephens Episcopal Mission for services conducted by Rev. Benjamin A. Rogers. He established the first non-denominational religious services in Houston Heights in 1895. The first floor of the east wing was the spacious dining room. Most rooms on the second floor rented for about $3.50 per week, the best rooms for $5.00 per week. Mr. Carter would stay at the hotel when he came to Houston Heights to check the progress of the development. D.D. Cooley, supervisor of development, had his office there also. The hotel operated until 1905 when it was leased to several doctors and became the Texas Christian Sanitarium. The structure was destroyed by fire on June 1, 1915. (Photograph courtesy of Houston Public Library, HMRC)

This view of 19th and Ashland Streets in 1893 shows where the business district of Houston Heights developed. The large building to the far left is Houston Heights Water Works. The brick building in the center, located at 406 W. 19th Avenue, was first operated as a general merchandise store by William C. McBride and also was the location of the first Heights post office, where Mr. McBride's wife, Irene, was the first Postmaster. This building, ten stores under one roof, was constructed for Mr. N. Merriam of Omaha, Nebraska, who purchased ten lots in May 1893. The brick building to the right of the McBride store was another general mercantile store located at 350 W. 19th Avenue and was operated by William Backus. The large, wooden structure to the right is the Houston Heights Hotel, constructed in 1892 to accommodate visitors and prospective buyers touring Houston Heights. When the hotel was put up for sale, an advertisement read " The Houston Heights Hotel together with beautiful grounds will be sold this week — the only ideal resort in or near Houston accessible by streetcar and macadamized (shell) road. A barrel of money can be made this season with increasing patronage each succeeding year — best cash offer accepted. John A. Milroy, agent, 220 Main Street." (Photograph courtesy of Houston Public Library, HMRC)

One of the many important improvements to Houston Heights before any lots were sold was the construction of Houston Heights Water Works located on 19th Avenue between Ashland and Railroad (Nicholson) Streets. The water works was completed on April 27, 1893, at a ceremony where Master Ralph C. Cooley, age 4, son of D.D. Cooley, turned the valve to set the machinery in motion. A dinner was held previously at the Houston Heights Hotel to celebrate the success of the Omaha and South Texas Land Company. The Houston Heights Water Works boasted of its artesian wells and a stand pipe for water storage which was 100 feet high and 20 feet in diameter, making it the second largest in the state. The company also had installed all water lines, sewer lines and fire plugs throughout Houston Heights. There was also a large public park area on the water works grounds which was used by Heights residents for many years. Today, the old fuel tank of the water works is the only remaining structure on the site. (Photograph courtesy of Houston Public Library, HMRC)

It was the intention of the developers of Houston Heights from the very beginning to attract major manufacturing concerns to guarantee economic stability and growth for the new community. The impressive list of manufacturers that located there speaks highly of the business abilities and connections of the planners of Houston Heights. In 1892, they also constructed a steam railroad line into the industrial area from a point where the Houston and Texas Central Railroad crossed Houston Heights. One business attracted to the area was the Oriental Textile Mill. In 1901, the company moved into the building previously occupied by the Houston Heights Spring Bed & Mattress Factory, which had located there in 1892. The mill manufactured yarns, textiles, fabrics and worsted goods for over 50 years and provided many jobs to Heights residents. At 22nd Avenue and Lowell Street (Shepherd), the company constructed several shotgun style houses in a four block area adjacent to the plant. The area became known as "Factory Village," where employees of the Oriental Textile Mill could live. Today the building is owned by Heights Industrial Center, which leases the building to W.R. Grace Company. (Photograph courtesy of Carter & Cooley Deli)

In the Fall of 1892, the Omaha and South Texas Land Company, developer of Houston Heights, opened the Houston Heights Real Estate Office at 211 Main Street in downtown Houston. N.L. Mills was superintendent of Real Estate. In that year, the company began selling 10,000 lots, but only after it had laid streets paved with shell, established alleys, water and sewer lines, electric light system, artesian wells, sidewalks and curbs along Heights Boulevard and constructed two twin bridges across White Oak Bayou. The company also laid the tracks for the streetcar so the community could be served by the electric streetcars of the Houston City Street Railway Company. In fact, so much activity had occurred since April that it inspired Clifford Grunewald to write the "Houston Heights Polka" which was dedicated to N.L. Mills. Later, John A. Milroy became superintendent of Real Estate and the office was located at 403 Main Street in the Scanlan Building shown here. Mr. Milroy is seated at the desk on the far left and O.M. Carter, who headed the development of Houston Heights, is seated at the desk on the far right. George S. Durant, a real estate agent who sold lots for the company, is probably one of the men in this photograph also. (Photograph courtesy Houston Public Library, HMRC)

Seventeen houses were built by the Omaha and South Texas Land Company, primarily on Heights Boulevard and Harvard Street. Of these, five became homes for Carter and his associates, D.D. Cooley, G.B. Hengen, John Milroy and N.L. Mills. All were fine, elaborate homes built from the plans of George Franklin Barber, an early Knoxville, Tennessee architect, who designed house plans and published them for sale through catalogues. He revolutionized the concept of house plans, giving individuals the ability to have a house designed by an architect without the cost of hiring one (in most cases and in many parts of the country, there were no architects to hire even if desired.) In fact, Barber did not just sell his plans "as is", but encouraged his clients to make suggestions, which he would incorporate into the plans they chose. All materials, including intricate millwork, could be ordered from the company and shipped via railroad. Shown here is the original home of N.L. Mills at 1530 Heights Boulevard, which later became the H.A. Paine residence in 1908. According to Sister Agatha's History of Houston Heights, this house was the most pretentious and highly decorative, with its intricate "gingerbread" fretwork. The house was razed in 1964. Of the original 17 houses, only three remain standing today — 1802 Harvard Street, 443 Heights Boulevard and 1102 Heights Boulevard. (Photograph courtesy of Houston Public Library, HMRC; history courtesy of Margaret Culbertson, librarian, Univ. of Houston, School of Architecture)

In 1892, the Omaha & South Texas Land Company began construction of many grand residences along Heights Boulevard. This home at 1102 Heights Boulevard was built in 1896 from the plans of architect, George F. Barber for H.F. MacGregor, although he never lived there. In 1896, John Milroy, the new superintendent of the Houston Heights Real Estate office moved into the house. He managed the office for over 18 years and sold lots in Houston Heights. He also served the City of Houston Heights as the second mayor and was re-elected seven times thereafter. In 1917, he opened his own real estate business and continued in that endeavor until his death on August 9, 1918. His daughter, Helen Milroy, lived in the home until her death, after which it was purchased by the present owners and restored. The home is currently a Registered Texas Historical Landmark and is listed in the National Register of Historic Places. (Photograph courtesy of Houston Public Library, HMRC)

Mr. Eden L. Coombs built this large home on Heights Boulevard in 1894 from the plans of architect George F. Barber. Mr. Coombs owned Sweeney, Coombs and Fredericks, a jewelry and watch company at 301 Main Street. He was also secretary of the Sweeney and Coombs Opera House at 316 Fannin Street. In 1893, Mr. Coombs began construction of the first park in Houston — a 50-acre "first class resort park in the flamboyant style of Coney Island." It was at the southeastern edge of Houston Heights where Harvard Street ends at White Oak Bayou. He immediately sunk an artesian well and built an artificial lake (known as the Natatorium) and ordered peafowls (peacocks) from Kentucky to wander the grounds. Coombs Park not only became the most popular recreational area to Heights residents, but also drew people from all over Houston (Houston had a population of 50,000, but no parks.) According to Sister Agatha's History of Houston Heights, Sunday afternoon was the park's biggest day. There was a track for goat racing and children would harness their pets to wagons, to take part in the race for prizes. Mr. Coombs also provided an ostrich farm and zoo with many species of animals for the children. Unfortunately for residents of Houston and Houston Heights, Coombs Park had a short life, as Mr. Coombs died in 1900. Except for the area occupied by the Natatorium, the remaining portion of Coombs Park was subdivided and sold as residential lots. (Photograph courtesy of Houston Public Library, HMRC)

William A. Wilson, of Syracuse, New York was one of the first investors to tour Houston Heights in 1892. He was so impressed with the city and its future that he moved here to live in 1893. He built many houses in Houston Heights and lived in a large home at 812 Heights Boulevard for several years. He was a member of the Houston Heights School Board in 1898 and was President of the Board of the Texas Christian Sanitarium in 1908. In 1907, he began development of Woodland Heights, a residential subdivision of the City of Houston much different from Houston Heights which was developed as a whole community of residences, businesses and manufacturing enterprises. He created the William A. Wilson Realty Company, bought 106 acres of land just east of Houston Heights, laid out 600 lots and built numerous homes in the bungalow style. Pictured here in 1907 are men clearing the land for the new subdivision. Wilson also developed the Eastwood subdivision just south of downtown Houston. He also published a magazine for several years called "Homes," which not only promoted his building projects but also contained articles oriented to the general interest of homeowners. In 1910, he built a large home for himself at 205 Bayland in Woodland Heights, where he lived until his death. Perhaps the most picturesque evidence of Wilson's work remaining today are the large oak trees that tent Bayland Avenue, his grand entrance into the neighborhood. (Photograph courtesy of Houston Public Library, HMRC)

The largest snowfall ever recorded in South Texas occurred on February 14, 1895. The City of Houston received 22 inches. According to the *Houston Daily Post*, the electric streetcar system was unable to operate and service had to be suspended for an entire day. For several hours, conductors and motormen remained with their cars, trying to get them through, finally having to abandon them where they stood. At 10 a.m., the entire streetcar line was completely abandoned and shortly thereafter, Superintendent Mundes (of the Houston City Street Railway Company) put out a force of men armed with shovels and brooms to clear the circuit at Main and Travis Streets. O.M. Carter said "such a snowstorm as we have just experienced would do credit to Maine." It was also reported that the streetcar which always remained in Houston Heights overnight, got as far as Chaneyville (Washington Avenue) but had to be abandoned as well. (Photograph courtesy of Houston Public Library, HMRC)

George Wickton Hawkins, who moved to Houston Heights in 1904, is shown here (seated on left) in Lansing, Michigan, where he traveled from Houston to purchase this 1902 Curved Dash Runabout. Known as the Oldsmobile, it was the world's first mass-produced automobile. Designed by Ransom Eli Olds, who founded the Olds Motor Works, the automobile was of a very short and simple buggy-type chassis with two long springs serving as auxiliary side-members, on which was mounted a single-cylinder 1.6 liter motor engine, with trembler coil ignition, a 2-speed epicycle transmission and central chain drive. The engine had an immense silencer and turned at 500 rpm - "one chug per telegraph pole." In 1902, G.W. Hawkins was to bring not one but many automobiles to Houston as president of the Hawkins Automobile and Gas Engine Co. The little Olds was an instant success — in 1902, U.S. sales totaled 2,100 units. Mr. Hawkins was issued Motor Vehicle License Plate No. 1. When James Ferguson became Governor of Texas in 1914, he insisted on having License Plate No. 1, so G.W. Hawkins relinquished that number and was issued License Plate No. 2. The tradition of governors having License Plate No. 1 has been continued since that time. Incidentally, Ferguson, while in office, created the Texas Highway Department. (Photograph courtesy of Mr. Grover C. Noonan Jr., grandson of G.W. Hawkins)

On Friday, November 21, 1902, the first horseless carriage (auto) parade in Houston's history was held during the annual NO-TSU-OH (Houston spelled backwards) carnival. There were 23 entries from seven different cities. G.W. Hawkins drove his 1902 Oldsmobile and was accompanied by his three daughters, Hazel, Cecil and Mae Hawkins. The automobile was covered with "white roses used in profusion" and won third prize in the parade. G.W. Hawkins is seated on the left, Mrs. Nettie Hawkins, his wife, is on the right and their youngest daughter, Mildred, is behind Mrs. Hawkins. G.W. Hawkins posed for the photograph in front of the old Rice Hotel on Texas Avenue to show off not only his floral car but a "sectional view" of the famous Oldsmobile on display at his dealership at 903 Texas Avenue. On November 24, 1903, another "first" occurred at the NO-TSU-OH event. The first auto races in the State of Texas were held "under horse racing rules." G.W. Hawkins was a member of the committee for the event. The out-of-town machines were on display in front of Hawkins' dealership. There were seven entries. During the first race, a bird dog ran out onto the track at Harrisburg and collided with Mr. Hawkins' Olds, driven by A.J. Sallers. The car struck the canine and careened off the track. Although Mr. Sallers managed to keep from being thrown from the car, the car received a "sprained axle" and the dog was fatally hurt. (Photograph courtesy of Mr. Grover C. Noonan Jr., grandson of G.W. Hawkins)

Harvard Street School, the second school in the area, opened its doors to children on the south end of Houston Heights on September 18, 1898. It was built on two lots at 8th and Harvard Streets and its school board included D.D. Cooley, W.G. Love, C.A. McKinney, John A. Milroy, L. Ream and William A. Wilson. Today it still serves as Harvard Elementary for the community in its original building and location. Pictured here is Miss Aline Sharp's third grade class of 1904. Garnett Robinson Smith is fifth from the right, second row. Living in Houston Heights since 1903, she was a member of the Neaubeaux Club (a social club for ladies and their beaus), the Mandolin Club and, later, a guiding force for the Heights Woman's Club, serving as president from 1969 to 1971. Garnett was adored by the entire community for her poetry, beautiful speeches and ladies' High Teas. (Photograph courtesy of Houston Public Library, Heights Branch collection)

Houston Heights High School at 12th and Yale Streets was erected in 1904. A. Hugh Russell was the first principal and Miss Lottie Burlingame was the first graduate in June 1905. Pictured here is the 9th grade class of 1908. The building became the Junior High School in 1921 when a new high school was built at 20th Avenue and Heights Boulevard, now known as Hamilton Junior High School. The original Houston Heights High School burned on March 13, 1924. Today, the site is known as Milroy Park, named in honor of John A. Milroy, one of Houston Heights' most prominent citizens. (Photograph courtesy of Houston Public Library, Heights Branch collection)

This 1910 photograph taken on 19th Avenue shows Heights Car No. 206. Frank Wisnoski, the first motorman on a streetcar to Houston Heights, is standing in the car. Outside, with his foot on the guard, is Conductor Sam Danna, the best-loved man on the Heights line. When he began working for the line in 1907, children would pass up other cars to wait to ride Danna's car. Once the Houston City Street Railway Company ran a popularity contest to choose the favorite streetcar conductor by printing coupons in the newspaper for readers to send in their votes. On February 1, 1913, Sam Danna won the contest over 49 other conductors. (Photograph courtesy Houston Public Library, Heights Branch collection)

Pictured here is 19th Avenue looking west from Heights Boulevard. The house on the right was located at 201 W. 19th Avenue and was the home of Ralph E. Bradshaw, who owned the R.E. Bradshaw Grain Company, located at 442 W. 19th Avenue. The house on the left, at 212 W. 19th Avenue, was the home of Reverend and Mrs. Henry J. Brown, who organized St. Andrews Episcopal Church in his home in February 1911. (Photograph courtesy of Houston Public Library, HMRC)

Correspondence dated December 9, 1909, written by Mrs. G.H.B. of Houston Heights reads "here is a handful of white Wyndotts. Wish our little cow was in the picture." In the early days of Houston Heights, there were no restrictions against cattle grazing any place in the community — and of course, none against any other kind of livestock. That changed however, when a stock law was passed in 1911 to keep cows from eating and trampling the more tender grass on the lawns of the fine homes. The law however, did not apply to chickens which could do almost as much damage to a flower or vegetable garden as even the wildest cow. As difficult as it was to pass the stock law, nothing could compare to what happened in 1913 when the residents forced owners to keep chickens in their coop. Robert C. Patterson, an attorney with Baker, Botts, Parker and Garwood, who lived at 1116 Columbia Street, resorted to his own method while waiting for the ordinance. He threaded tags, on long strings, through fat kernels of corn. The tags read "keep your confounded chickens at home." The chickens would swallow the corn and then the string, but when they could not swallow the tag, they would return home, squawking and fluttering until freed from the tags by their owners. Although some chickens' owners did not like the lesson taught, eventually, the chicken law passed. (Photograph courtesy of Carter & Cooley Deli)

"This is papa and one of our horses'" wrote Fern Everhart of Houston Heights in 1909 to her brother, Frank Everhart of Marcus, Iowa. Charles R. Everhart, their father, was proprietor of Alamo Livery, Sale and Transfer Barn, located at 520 W. 19th Avenue between Railroad (Nicholson) and Lawrence Streets. Mr. Everhart was also Deputy City Marshall of Houston Heights in 1910. In 1912, he was in partnership with Wilbur N. Mateer, a veterinarian surgeon, to provide livery, boarding, sales, stable, veterinarian hospital and transfer line to the many residents of Houston Heights. The advertisement on the wagon reads, "Phone 643 Alamo Transfer Barn, Houston Heights." (Photograph courtesy of Carter & Cooley Deli)

When the members of the Houston Heights Woman's Club decided to build a clubhouse on the lot donated to them by Mrs. Helen Cooley, the women held a carnival in 1911 to raise money for the building. The carnival was held on the Heights playground, now the site of Hamilton Junior High School. The club also held benefit plays to raise money. Most were organized, produced and directed by Mrs. Myrtle Cook Lowery, one of the Heights' most beloved citizens, who graduated from her early home theatricals to become a nationally famous actress. On September 13, 1912, the Houston Heights Woman's Club met for the first time in their newly constructed clubhouse at 1846 Harvard Street. The club's first president was Mrs. W.A. Renn. Its opening celebration and dedication took place on October 18, 1912 and the guests of honor were Mr. and Mrs. D.D. Cooley. Scarcely one year after the land was donated, the members of the club had managed to furnish the clubhouse and completely pay off the debt of $1,500 owed for its construction. The clubhouse has been used by its members continuously to the present time. Today, it is owned and maintained by the Houston Heights Association and is listed in the National Register of Historic Places. (Photograph courtesy of Houston Public Library, Heights branch)

The Houston Heights Literary Club was organized in 1899 as the first organization for women in Houston Heights. In addition to its literary studies, the group became well known for its work among the poor. The club, however, quickly outgrew its single interest and other "departments," such as the Arts and Crafts Club and the Music Club were created. By 1911, the Literary Club had expanded into enough departments to incorporate itself into a more general title of Woman's Club. The members of the Houston Heights Woman's Club were dedicated to their projects and activities as exemplified by the accomplishment of the construction of their own clubhouse. Pictured here on the lawn of the W.A. Renn Home at 1007 Heights Boulevard are members of the Houston Heights Music Club (one of the groups that merged, becoming the Music Department of the Houston Heights Woman's Club.) Before the clubhouse was built, all groups met at the homes of their members. The two older women seated in the middle of the second row were two charter members of the Houston Heights Woman's Club — Mrs. D.D. Cooley (left) and Mrs. W.B. Welling (right). After the clubhouse was built, the Music Department purchased a piano for the clubhouse at a cost of $1,500 (the same as the cost for construction of the clubhouse.) (Photograph courtesy of Houston Public Library, HMRC)

Streetcars began running to Houston Heights on October 23, 1892, after the American Loan & Trust Company electrified the streetcar system of Houston. The cars ran up the east side of Heights Boulevard from Washington Avenue and turned west on 19th Avenue, to the Houston Heights Hotel on Ashland Street. On March 31, 1893, the loop down to Railroad (Nicholson) Street was completed where the cars turned south, then east on 17th Avenue and back to Heights Boulevard, where they turned south and proceeded down the west side of Heights Boulevard and back to Washington Avenue. As the industrial section of Houston Heights expanded, the streetcars could not travel down Nicholson because boxcars loaded with manufactured goods would frequently block the tracks. Therefore, the streetcar line was laid on Ashland Street between 19th and 17th Avenues to allow the system open tracks at all times. The Houston Heights line was one of the most popular and most heavily traveled in the City of Houston. It was the last line to be discontinued when the streetcar form of transportation was abandoned on April 27, 1940, to make way for the "more progressive system of buses." (Photograph courtesy of Parsley Studios)

Built about 1896, the Heights Natatorium was located in the old Coombs Park at the end of Harvard Street at White Oak Bayou. The building had open galleries two and a half stories tall that surrounded and overlooked the water. Dressing rooms were located on each floor. The entrance was flanked by a large round tower and two smaller turrets on which flags were mounted. According to Sister Agatha's <u>History of Houston Heights</u>, the original building burned early on and a more modest structure was erected (pictured here.) When Coombs Park was dismantled, the Natatorium was also sold, eventually to the Vieweger family in 1907, who ran it for many years. Its last owners were Mrs. Beulah Dean and Charles H. Dean Jr., who operated it from 1929 until 1942. For years it was a drawing card to the Heights before swimming pools existed and was perhaps the most popular Heights attraction for young and old alike. This photograph was taken by Hawthorne Ramage about 1913. (Photograph donated by Ms. Verna Topkins to Heights Museum Collection)

Baptist Temple had its beginning in 1908 when it was organized at 411 W. 19th Avenue over the Thomas J. Rutledge Grocery Store, also the site of the fourth post office in Houston Heights. The Reverend Fred Huhns was pastor. The first Heights library opened its doors on June 29, 1909 over the same store. Although organized by the Baptist Temple, the library was open to everyone, and the entire community supported the endeavor. In 1912, a new brick building was constructed on land donated by O.M. Carter at 20th and Rutland Streets. Pictured here in 1915 is the congregation attending a Sunday service. (Photograph courtesy of Houston Public Library, HMRC)

Judge Thomas Martin Kennerly with his Baptist Temple Sunday School class on the porch of his home at 1523 Heights Boulevard in 1917. The home was designed by architect, A.D. Steele, and built in 1915. The Kennerly family and guests spent many warm days in the cool shade of the summer house (pictured left), which was covered with wysteria vines and climbing roses. T.M. Kennerly was one of the founders of Baptist Temple and was an instrumental sponsor in the establishment of the first library in Houston Heights. (Photograph courtesy of Thomas Martin Kennerly)

D.D. Cooley, seated on the left, is shown here with his wife, Helen Winfield Cooley, and their three sons (left to right) Ralph Clarkson Cooley, Denton Winfield Cooley and Arthur Waugh Cooley. D.D. Cooley came to Houston in 1890 to oversee the development of Houston Heights. He was instrumental in the development of Heights Boulevard, which remains his great memorial. In December 1892, just before Christmas, he was presented with a gold and ebony cane. It was given to him as a gift of appreciation and inscribed "From the Boys," namely O.M. Carter, C.A. McKinney and others of the Omaha and South Texas Land Company. Concerned about education, Cooley deeded land, through the Omaha and South Texas Land Company, to Harris County for the first school in Houston Heights. The school was named in Mr. Cooley's honor. Mrs. Cooley was also the first president of the Mother's Club of Cooley School when it was established in 1907. It was a practice of Mr. Cooley to give lots to Mrs. Cooley on her birthdays and anniversaries. One of those lots was donated by Mrs. Cooley for the Houston Heights Woman's Club and became the site for the clubhouse in 1912. Both Mr. and Mrs. Cooley remained active in Houston Heights' business and social affairs until their deaths. (Photograph donated by Talbot Cooley, grandson of Ralph C. Cooley, to Heights Museum Collection)

Prize Winning Roadster, Floral Parade, Deep Water Jubilee, Houston, 1914.

Dr. Ralph C. Cooley poses proudly in front of the Cooley home with his prize-winning roadster of the Floral Parade. The Deep Water Jubilee was held November 9-14th, 1914, to celebrate the opening of the Houston Ship Channel in conjunction with the NO-TSU-OH (Houston spelled backwards) annual carnival. Part of the celebration was the Floral Parade, held on November 12th. Dr. Cooley entered his car in the roadster category in the parade and won first place. Other decorated parade vehicles included touring cars, electric and coup automobiles, floats and motorcycles. The NO-TSU-OH celebration had been held since 1899 in Houston. It was staged by the NO-TSU-OH Society, a mystic circle of 400 to 500 Houston businessmen and citizens. Each year a King and Queen reigned over the festivities. In 1914, those selected were Eugene A. Hudson, King Retaw I and Miss Fannie Carter, Queen NO-TSU-OH. (Photograph donated Talbot Cooley, grandson of Ralph C. Cooley, to Heights Museum Collection)

The Durham family moved to Houston Heights after losing all their worldly possessions in the great hurricane that devastated Galveston Island in 1900. The Durhams built their first home at 921 Heights Boulevard. After the family outgrew their home, they moved to 1201 Heights Boulevard. In 1910, Mr. Durham became the first paid fire chief when the City of Houston Heights established a tax-supported fire department (it had been voluntary up to that point.) Pictured here in 1915 is Mr. & Mrs. J.L. Durham and their six children out for a Sunday drive, a popular activity for the many young families living in Houston Heights. The original Durham home at 921 Heights Boulevard is one of a number of homes in Houston Heights listed in the National Register of Historic Places. Today the home is known as Durham House Bed and Breakfast. (Photograph donated by Ms. Mary Anelda Peterson, youngest daughter of J.L. Durham)

The first tax-supported fire department was established in 1910 on 12th Avenue and Heights Boulevard, behind the Durham home. The station opened into the alley between Heights Boulevard and Yale Street. J.L. Durham was the first paid fire chief and his firemen were Lee Nixon, Lee Butler and Mr. Haxthausen. When Fraternal Hall, the town's community center at 12th and Yale Streets, burned in 1912, a combination city hall, jail and fire station was built on that site in 1914. The architect for the building was Alonzo C. Pigg. On March 1, 1915, Hugh Montgomery was appointed fire chief for Houston Heights. His new crew included Captain M.T. Robinson, Lieutenant Ed Kohlman and pipe and laddermen G.K. Parker, O. M. Phillips, Roy Crush, S. Lowe and E. Hueboetter. The building has changed little since this early photograph and still serves the Heights community as the local fire station. (Photograph courtesy of Houston Fire Museum through HMRC)

Fire Station No. 13 on 18th and Rutland Streets grew as an extension of the central fire station on 12th and Yale Streets. The building pictured here had served previously as the town jail. Sitting in the fire truck in both photographs is Edwin "Big Ed" Kohlman who served as an officer in the Heights Fire Department before Houston Heights was annexed by the City of Houston. Kohlman was born in Houston's Sixth Ward and moved to 801 Rutland Street in the 1890s. He joined the Houston Heights Fire Department as a young boy and by 1915 was a lieutenant, assigned to the 18th Avenue station. This small station housed a pumper, a kitchen area and sleeping quarters for the five- or six-man crew. "Big Ed" worked his way up through the ranks, eventually becoming a training chief of the Houston Fire Department, before he died in 1934 at age 42. Although no longer used as a fire station, the building still stands and serves as an office. (Photograph courtesy of the Kohlman family)

Clayton Lee came to Houston Heights with his new bride in 1910. After traveling around the country as an independent plumber, Clayton settled in Houston, buying his first house at 420 E. 24th Avenue. Opening his doors for business at that location when the local Plumbers Union went on strike, his business immediately flourished. In 1921, Clayton moved his wife and two children, Clayton Jr. and Anna Doris, to a new home at 706 E. 20th Avenue, building his shop in the backyard. The business eventually expanded to include the property next door at 704 E. 20th Avenue, which he purchased in 1930 for $1,394.35. When Clayton died in 1938, Clayton, Jr. took over the business, and became the youngest master plumber in the State of Texas, receiving his journeyman and master plumber's license at age 19. Clayton Lee Plumbing, now located in the old J.E. Banta Candy Factory at 101 E. 20th Avenue, is operated by a member of the third- generation, Clayton Lee III. Pictured here is Clayton Lee with his daughter, Anna Doris, about 1917. (Photograph courtesy of Clayton Lee Jr.)

In 1912 polish immigrant Dave Kaplan, leased the F.F. Ibsch store at 22nd and Yale Streets, then on the fringe of Houston Heights. Two years later, Kaplan moved across the street into his own establishment, a wooden building with living quarters upstairs. The store initially sold groceries, meat and feed, and the Kaplans would deliver groceries to local residents in a mule-drawn wagon. In 1924, the building was expanded and the spaces on either side leased to other businesses, the first one being Yale Drug Store pictured here. Eventually, the Kaplans added piece goods to their inventory, and the feed and grocery business was eliminated gradually. By the 1920s, the store sold primarily dry goods. Kaplan's two sons, Herman and Bennett, virtually grew up in the store. After graduating from Rice University in the 1930s, Herman continued to work at the store and in 1939, Bennett began his own variety store in one of the side spaces. The store, named "Ben Hur" after the two brothers, made a pivotal expansion during World War II to include a wider selection of merchandise, similar to the store's inventory today. Although the building has been updated and expanded more than six times over the past 75 years, Kaplan's Ben Hur is still run by third-generation family members and remains a neighborhood landmark. (Photograph: Houston Public Library, Heights Branch collection)

Yale Pharmacy, founded by Abel J. and Mildred (Grambling) Dupuis in 1923, was located at 2219 Yale Street. Shortly thereafter, it relocated to the Dave Kaplan Building on 22nd and Yale Streets, where the Dupuis' leased space in the newly expanded building. The photograph on the left shows the interior of this store. Abel and Mildred remained at that location until 1928 when they built their first store, at 2136 Yale Street. Shown in the photograph on the right is the new store, taken around New Years, as evidenced by the tinsel hung around the walls and fire crackers on the table. Pictured in the middle is Abel Dupuis wearing his white pharmacist jacket, and to the right of Abel, behind the fountain was the Dupuis' fountain employee and "Car Hop." The Yale fountain featured malted milks, banana splits and ice cream cones. However, the Dupuis' had the only fountain around that featured curbside service. Patrons, served by the Car Hop, could sit in their car, eat their ice cream and listen to the Dupuis' radio perched on the ledge. When their son A.J., Jr. became a pharmacist, they decided to build at their present location, 2100 Yale Street. The store opened in 1952 and is still owned and operated by the Dupuis family. Mildred Dupuis, who is still active in the business, became the first woman pharmacist in the State of Texas in 1926. (Photograph courtesy of the Dupuis family)

At the end of the 1920 football season, Heights (better known as "Hites") High School became the state football champion — however, the school shared the title with Cleburne High School. According to The Pennant (Heights High School's yearbook), the team waded through the hardest schedule of football ever. Hites High was put on the map of Texas by winning state honors with Cleburne, giving the team the notoriety that only comes to a good school with a good football team, the yearbook said. The last game of the season played against Cleburne was at the University of Texas in Austin in a sea of mud before a crowd of 4,000. Both teams went into the final game undefeated. The final score — 0 to 0 resulted in a tie for the state championship. (Photograph courtesy of Houston Public Library, HMRC)

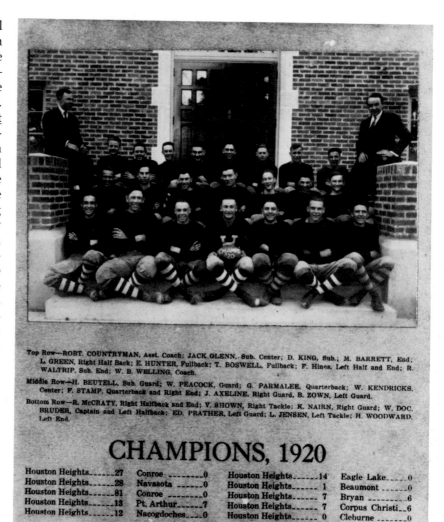

Top Row—ROBT. COUNTRYMAN, Asst. Coach; JACK GLENN, Sub. Center; D. KING, Sub.; M. BARRETT, End; L. GREEN, Right Half Back; E. HUNTER, Fullback; T. BOSWELL, Fullback; F. Hines, Left Half and End; R. WALTRIP, Sub. End; W. B. WELLING, Coach.

Middle Row—H. BEUTELL, Sub. Guard; W. PEACOCK, Guard; G. PARMALEE, Quarterback; W. KENDRICKS, Center; F. STAMP, Quarterback and Right End; J. AXELINE, Right Guard, B. ZOWN, Left Guard.

Bottom Row—R. McCRATY, Right Halfback and End; V. SHOWN, Right Tackle; K. NAIRN, Right Guard; W. DOC. BRUDER, Captain and Left Halfback; ED. PRATHER, Left Guard; L. JENSEN, Left Tackle; H. WOODWARD, Left End.

CHAMPIONS, 1920

Houston Heights	27	Conroe	0	Houston Heights	14	Eagle Lake	0
Houston Heights	28	Navasota	0	Houston Heights	1	Beaumont	0
Houston Heights	81	Conroe	0	Houston Heights	7	Bryan	6
Houston Heights	13	Pt. Arthur	7	Houston Heights	7	Corpus Christi	6
Houston Heights	12	Nacogdoches	0	Houston Heights	0	Cleburne	0

In 1926, John R. Reagan High School was constructed at 401 E. 13th Avenue. The entire student body is seen here marching down Heights Boulevard to the new school from their former high school which then became Hamilton Junior High School. Hamilton was built in 1921 at 20th Avenue and Heights Boulevard as the new high school and the original Heights High School at 12th and Yale Streets became the junior high school. The latter burned on March 13, 1924, prompting the construction of Reagan, which was design by the famous architect, John R. Staub. (Photograph courtesy of Houston Public Library, Heights Branch collection)

Heights Christian Church, founded May 13, 1912, began in a room of the F.F. Dexter Grocery Store, at the corner of 17th and Rutland Streets. There were 24 charter members, one of whom was Dr. Thomas Sinclair, founder of Heights Hospital. In 1913, three lots where purchased on 16th and Rutland Streets and the first Tabernacle was erected. The congregation worshipped at that location until 1927 when they constructed the present church at 16th Avenue and Heights Boulevard. Pictured here on Easter Sunday, April 7, 1928, is the Heights Christian Church Sunday school class — better known as the "Cradle Roll." (Photograph courtesy of Houston Public Library, HMRC)

Charles S. Stratton, a famous American midget who lived from 1838 until 1883, was better known under his circus name — "General Tom Thumb." A dwarf, he was only 40 inches tall and weighed 70 pounds as an adult. He traveled the globe with Barnum-Bailey Circus for many years, entertaining people wherever he went. In 1863, he married Lavinia Warren, another Barnum midget and the wedding made big headlines throughout the world. Pictured here is a staged, "Tom Thumb Wedding", which was performed in Heights Christian Church's auditorium in the late 1920s by some of the church's youngest members. Wedding participants were Paul Porter, minister, Doris Walker, bride, and Bill Adams, groom. Bridesmaids were Doris Walters, Jennette Schrister and Kathrine Grechel. Flower girls were Lucile Aldridge and Caroline Hill. The event was performed only one time for the enjoyment of the church's members. (Photograph courtesy of Heights Christian Church)

John H. Reagan Masonic Lodge No. 1037, Heights Chapter No. 258 OES A.F. and A.M., was chartered on December 12, 1910, and met in the volunteer fire department building next to Dr. William Olive's Drugs at 910 Yale Street. Charter members pictured here included James F. Helm, W.H. Ward, C.C. Hart, R.J. Shallcross, Emil G. Detrich, Dr. William Olive, William O. Backus, C.I. Voss, Ed White, V.B. Watson, O.C. Grubb, P.L. Cooper, Clayton Lee and A. Cameron Bernard. (Photograph courtesy of Houston Public Library, Heights Branch collection)

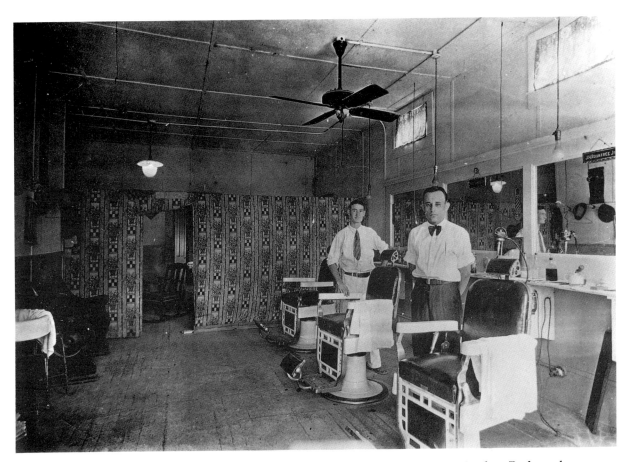

Barber shops, like other personal service businesses, were abundant in Houston Heights. Barbers shops were places for the menfolk to socialize, visit and catch up on the local news. Taken about 1929, this photograph shows Sixteenth Avenue Barber Shop, located at 1601 Lawrence Street. Pictured are W.A. Cones Jr. and J.H. Roundtree Jr., who worked for the owner, Mr. W.A. Cones. He operated the shop from 1928 until 1940. Both employees also opened their own shops before this shop closed — Roundtree opened his shop around the corner at 601 W. 16th Avenue and Cones opened his shop in Humble, Texas. (Photograph courtesy of Houston Public Library, Heights Branch collection)

William, James and Stonewall Jackson Wimberly came to Houston Heights in the late 1890s from Tennessee. Shortly thereafter, the three brothers built the first Wimberly Store, a small wooden structure, located at 7th Avenue and Heights Boulevard. The store carried general merchandise and feed, and a few years later added the first neighborhood gas pump. As business grew, the Wimberlys rebuilt the store as a brick structure in the 1920s. The newly designed Wimberly Store introduced the concept of "self-serve" grocery shopping, one of the first in Houston at that time. The new store also leased space to Ezzels Drug Store, on the far right side of the building. Pictured here, shortly after the store was built, is Carter (son of William), James and William Wimberly, second, third and fifth from left, and the Ezzels at the far right. The store operated until the Great Depression. The property sat vacant for nearly three decades until the Houston Heights Association, through a grant from Houston Endowment, purchased the site to prevent the development of a tractor-trailer repair facility in 1979. Today it is the site of Donovan Park, and is owned and maintained by the Houston Heights Association. It was named in honor of James G. Donovan, the last city attorney of Houston Heights, who drafted the "dry ordinance" in 1912, which remains in effect "until time runeth not." (Photograph donated by Glen Trupper (fourth from right) to the Heights Museum Collection)

Watts Feed Store was located at 545 W. 19th Avenue. Shown from left to right is Octavia Watts, William E. Watts, her husband, "Red" Follis, Bobby Reynolds, Espy Watts (son of Octavia and William) and Lee Willingham. The Watts moved to Houston Heights in 1931 and were in partnership with A.L. Smalley at the 19th Avenue Grain and Fuel Company. In 1945, the Watts opened their own store, which sold feed and supplies for cows, pigs and chickens to their many Heights customers. Because they sold "Egg-A-Day Feed" for chickens, the Houston company painted huge eggs all over the building to advertise their product. The Watts lost their lease in 1946 but moved their successful business to 620 W. 19th Avenue where they operated the store until the death of Mr. Watts in 1948. (Photograph courtesy of Octavia Watts Lemon)

Pictured here is Coach Turgeson's junior high school basketball team of 1933, taken outside their alma mater, Hamilton Junior High School (formerly Heights Senior High School) at 20th Avenue and Heights Boulevard. Holding the basketball is Jake Wilke and seated, second from the right, is Bill Henderson, better known as "Jitterbug" to his classmates at Reagan High School and Texas A&M. "Jitterbug" went on to be a great athlete at Texas A&M University, where he won 11 varsity letters in five sports (football, basketball, baseball, track and heavyweight boxing) during his college career. In 1964, he was inducted as a charter member of the Texas A&M Athletic Hall of Fame. (Photograph donated by Bob Bailey Studios to Heights Museum Collection)

May Day (May 1) is celebrated as a spring festival in many countries, marking the revival of life in early spring after winter. Some believe that celebrations of May Day go back to the spring festivals of ancient Egypt and India. The Romans developed their May Day celebrations to honor the goddess of springtime, Flora and celebrated the festival of Floralia. In medieval times, May Day became the favorite holiday of many English villages. People gathered spring flowers to decorate their homes and churches. They sang spring carols and chose a King and Queen of May. In Italy, boys serenaded their sweethearts. In Switzerland, a May pine tree was placed under a girl's window. In France, young girls as May queens, led processions in honor of the Virgin Mary. The Puritans however, frowned on May Day, and for this reason, the day has never been celebrated with as much enthusiasm in the United States as in other countries. However, in many American towns and cities, children celebrate the return of spring by dancing around the Maypole, singing May Day songs and selecting May Day Kings and Queens. Pictured here in 1937 is Hamilton Junior High School's King and Queen of "May Fete." From left to right is Tom Sinclair, Bernice Owens, Pat McMichael (King), Helen Burk (Queen), Bob Hart, Barbara Graham, Billy Stroud, and Mariam Ormarod. (Photograph courtesy of Jim McMichael)

Yale Theater located on the corner of Yale Street and Washington Avenue, opened May 21, 1938, with the feature film, <u>Navy Blue and Gold</u>, starring James Stewart. The theater was part of the national chain, Interstate Theaters. Ads described it as "Interstate's newest suburban theater, with streamlined Airtex seats, new air conditioning and Western Electric Wide Range Sound." Seats were 5¢, 10¢ and 25¢ and a "Popeye Club" attracted children. The theater was razed in the mid 1960s to make room for the new Heights State Bank building. (Photograph donated to Heights Museum by Bob Bailey Studios)

The first Heights Theatre, built by Simon Lewis in 1922, was originally at the corner of 19th and Ashland Streets. The theater opened in 1925 in a small storefront with 350 folding chairs, screen and projector. The new theater was built in 1929 by Charles Wygant who moved its location to the middle of the block. The building, originally constructed in the mission style of architecture, seated more than 500. The interior was of the Spanish colonial influence (pictured here). Opening day, May 14, 1929, featured Zane Grey's silent western, Sunset Pass. Charles Wygant leased the building to his son, Robert and then to his grandson, Richard, until 1957. Less than ten years after its construction, the theater underwent a major renovation. Updates included: a total change of the facade to a "deco" style of architecture; interior altered from a Spanish colonial to a plush Americana; addition of a basement to house the new air conditioning unit (reportedly the first in Houston) and expansion of the building to increase seating by more than 400. The theater ran special promotions which attracted people from all over the city — gangster movies featured beat-up, bullet-ridden cars, parked out front; Tarzan movies would feature caged live lions or tigers, and occasionally, movie stars such as Gene Autrey, would visit the theater on opening night. The Heights Theater's motto was "Home Owned and Operated by Heights People." (Photographs donated by Bob Bailey Studios (exterior) and Richard Wygant (interior))

The modern oil industry was born in 1901 with the discovery of the Spindletop Field near Beaumont. This field overlayed a salt dome which became the primary drilling target in the Gulf Coast through the 1930s. Geophysical methods first put to use in Texas in 1924 proved highly successful in locating these salt domes. The Eureka Heights Field, discovered in 1934 by C.B. Bunte, was among the early successes for these new techniques. The area spanned south of 18th Avenue to 12th Avenue and White Oak Bayou. By the end of 1938, 21 wells were producing in the field. This promotional shot of the "Heights Oil Well" was taken on March 20, 1939, for Hughes Tool Company. Ultimately, more than 50 wells were drilled in the area, with more than 40 proving productive. Eureka Heights Field produced more than 7.2 million barrels of oil before being depleted. All that remains in the area of the old field are abandoned production facilities located just south of the intersection of Bevis and W. 18th Avenue. (Photograph donated by Bob Bailey Studios; History courtesy of Robert Killian)

"No blaze is too big or stubborn for Pat Patton, one-armed master of the hazardous business of fire-fighting," said a 1946 article in <u>Coronot Magazine</u> about H.L. "Pat" Patton. Patton launched his career by accident in 1929 when he volunteered to put out a fierce fire in an oil field of Old London, Texas, which had already killed three firefighters. A trucking operator, Patton's fame as a firefighter spread quickly through Texas and then to every oil field in the United States. His guarantee — "If I don't cap the fire, you don't owe me a penny." The article tells of his bloodiest battle at Vermillion Bay in New Iberia, where a blazing well exploded, blowing debris skyward and killing his brother, Will Patton, and crewman Ed Richardson. A piece of flying metal sheared Pat Patton's arm to the bone. He was rushed to the hospital, where his arm was amputated near the shoulder. Patton was back five days later to defeat the fire. His greatest challenge, however, was when he put out the largest 12 of 37 oil-well fires set by the Japanese before they fled Borneo in 1945. Patton's two inventions—the "seating tool" and "fire-pan shield," coupled with his strategy of keeping a fleet of trucks and tractors dispersed in various areas, and his personally designed asbestos suits and goggles made him world famous. He moved to Houston Heights in the early 1920s and lived at 1319 Heights Boulevard (pictured here) from 1933 until 1948, when he retired to to his 800-acre ranch. He died February 20, 1989, at the age of 100 years and 20 days. (Photograph courtesy of Houston Public Library, Heights Branch)

SANDY

HOLE DE LA SWIM

Swimming holes on White Oak Bayou were abundant and quite popular among the boys in the neighborhood. Sandy swimming hole, shown here as it looked in the 1930s, was fondly remembered by oil well fire fighter, Red Adair, as a place he frequented as a boy. It was located on White Oak Bayou where Studewood Park is today. (Photograph courtesy of H.E. Swinney through Houston Heights Tribune)

The top photograph is of the interior of Ward's 19th Avenue Drugs at 19th and Ashland Streets in 1938. Pat Morrison, seated at one of the marble top tables, was a prescription delivery boy and soda jerk for Mr. Ward. The bottom photograph shows Maurice T. Ward and Pat Morrison making a prescription delivery on their horses. According to Dr. Thomas Sinclair, the best malts were made at Ward's Drugs. Other hardworking soda jerks at that time were J.P. Wilkinson, Walter L. Williford and Harold E. Sweeney. The building that housed Ward's Drugs was constructed by Simon Lewis in 1921 and it was leased to Treadwell-Roland Drug Company. The offices of Dr. E.E. Grant, Dr. G.J. Robinson, and Dr. Paul Kittel Jr., dentist, were above the store. In 1923, Fonville Drug Company No. 2 opened here and operated until Maurice Ward opened his store in 1926. Mr. Ward and his family later lived above the store in 1931 and continued their business until his death in 1964. Today, the site is the location of Carter & Cooley Deli, whose interior restoration reflects the charm of the old drugstore days. (Photograph courtesy of Harold E. Swinney, former soda jerk)

By 1928, Humble Oil & Refining Company had constructed four service stations in Houston. In 1929, the company expanded the number to 17, including station #141 at 122 W. 19th Avenue in Houston Heights. The station was first operated by Jack Standard, followed by Larry Doyle in 1932. The station was razed in 1989. John F. Staub had been commissioned to design a series of service stations for the company, which embarked on an ambitious plan to expand its retail service centers. Mr. Staub designed two styles, one octagonal and the other rectangular with pyramidal pediments in the center of each wall, decorative colored tile cornices and pitched copper roofs. Mr. Staub was also architect for Reagan High School and numerous other prominent buildings and residences in Houston. (Photograph courtesy of Carter & Cooley Deli)

The first Heights Hospital, located at 1919 Ashland Street between 19th and 20th Avenues, was built in 1924. Dr. Thomas A. Sinclair started a modern building program that year, adding an operating room, dining room, kitchen, five patients' rooms and a suite of four offices, including those of Dr. M.E. Durham and Dr. Paul Knittel, a dentist. By 1941, the hospital had been expanded to 40 patient rooms and a capacity of 50 beds. Mrs. Ella Ward began training program for nurses at Heights Hospital. Her husband, Maurice T. Ward, operated a pharmacy across from the hospital. The present Heights Hospital building was constructed on the same site. (Photograph courtesy of Parsley Studios)

Heights residents celebrate the Golden Jubilee in 1941, to honor Houston Heights' 50th anniversary. The event was held on the esplanade of Heights Boulevard at 13th Avenue. According to an article that appeared in the May 9th issue of the *Heights Citizen*, 20,000 people took part in the celebration which began with an afternoon parade and ended at 10:30 p.m with a two-hour speakers program and crowning of a Golden Jubilee king and queen. Miss Gertrude Grant, an 18 year-old Reagan high school graduate, was crowned "Queen of Today" by Mrs. Inger Moller, 77, who was crowned "Queen of Yesteryear." Mrs. Moller, a native of Denmark, came to the Heights in 1891 when the area was first being developed. Another Reagan graduate, Kenneth Walrod, was crowned "King of the Heights Golden Jubilee." (Article donated to Heights Museum Collection by C.W. Keith; Photograph courtesy of Houston Public Library, HMRC)

J.B. Marmion Jr., son of the last mayor of Houston Heights, J.B. Marmion, owned and operated a small Sinclair service station on the northwest corner of 19th and Yale Streets, from 1933 until 1949. He then moved his business to the northeast corner in the same block and built a new eight-gas-pump station. A new television was given away at the new station's grand opening in 1949. J.B., Jr. operated the station until his retirement in 1969. Pictured at the station's opening is J.B., Jr., pumping gas for this vintage Model T Ford automobile. (Photographs donated by Bob Bailey Studios to Heights Museum Collection)

Harold's Men's Wear at 350 W. 19th Avenue, was founded by Emmanuel Wiesenthal and his two sons, Harold and Milton. The store opened in 1950 in a 1,200-square-foot building built by Emmanuel at the corner of 19th and Ashland Streets. Growth came steadily, which prompted the Wiesenthals in 1980 to purchase Sammy's Cafe, a local landmark next door, subdividing it into more floor space. Today, the store, still at the same location, is a series of connected rooms which totals more than 15,000 square feet. Harold's remains one of the city's premier men's stores. Their customers include oil sheiks, sports stars, politicians and entertainers. Today, the business includes two new partners — Harold's sons Darryl and Michael. Pictured here in 1950 (from left to right) are Emmanuel Wiesenthal, C.W. ("House Doctor") McLemore, Harold and Milton Wiesenthal. (Photograph courtesy of Houston Public Library, Heights Branch collection)

On March 19, 1991, the Houston Heights community lost a dear friend and devoted patron with the passing of Milton Wiesenthal. He was a resident, as well as a businessman, in the Heights for many years. In addition to being a founder of the Houston Heights Association, he was a driving force behind the development of the Heights Main Street Project and eventual formation of the Greater Heights Area Chamber of Commerce. Above all else, he will be remembered for his unyielding faith and determination to bring about the rebirth of Houston Heights. He will be deeply missed by his many friends and colleagues.

Heights Savings Association was founded in 1953 by James G. Donovan, the last city attorney for the City of Houston Heights. Heights Savings was an important institution to the Heights community for many years. Its Board of Directors consisted of a "cross section of outstanding Heights area and Houston businessmen." Marcella Perry, formerly a dancer, teacher and resident of Heights Boulevard, was secretary-treasurer before succeeding her father, James Donovan, as president, in 1961. Ms. Perry, the only woman president of the 19th Avenue Association (merchants association) was a leader in the community and instrumental in the revitalization of the Houston Heights community. She was one of the founders of the Houston Heights Association in 1973. This photograph was taken on May 4, 1954, at the opening of Heights Savings Association at 233 W. 19th Avenue. Pictured left to right is James Donovan, Congressman Bob Casey, Marcella Perry and Mayor Roy Hofheinz. (Photograph courtesy of Marcella Donovan Perry)

Constructed in 1892-3, the Cooley mansion was one of the first houses built in Houston Heights by the Omaha and South Texas Land Company. D.D. Cooley, a descendant of early English settlers of Massachusetts, came here from Nebraska as the treasurer and promoter of the Omaha and South Texas Land Company. The house stood on a 1/2-acre lot at 18th Avenue and Heights Boulevard. When the electric trolley lines were installed on the Boulevard, D.D. Cooley connected the electric lines to his house, making it one of the first in the Heights to have the modern convenience of electricity. Mr. and Mrs. D.D. Cooley were the parents of three sons, Denton, Arthur and Ralph. After his father died in 1933, Arthur continued to live in the house. After Arthur's death in 1962, the grandsons, Ralph Jr. and Dr. Denton Cooley, were unsuccessful in selling the house at an asking price of $45,000. Eventually the grandsons were forced to sell it to Olshan Demolishing Company, who dismantled it and sold the remnants. Pictured here is the Cooley house in October 1965, a few months before it was demolished. The lot where the Cooley house once stood remained vacant until 1979 when it was purchased by the Houston Heights Association for the purpose of constructing Marmion Park, named in honor of the last mayor of Houston Heights, J.B. Marmion. The park's award-winning Kaiser Pavilion was designed to emulate the Cooley home's unique turret. (Photograph courtesy of Houston Public Library, HMRC)

The Wygant family closed the doors to the Heights Theatre in January 1957, due to declining profits, much of which was attributed to the popularity of television. In 1958, the Wygants sold the building to John Scott and W.E. Coats Jr. who updated the building and reopened on April 18, 1959 with <u>April Love</u>, starring Pat Boone as the feature film. Although the Scotts owned the building, they leased the theater to another movie house and subsequently, the "moral content of films changed drastically from what had been the industry standard." R- and X-rated films cropped up, including the controversial Swedish film, <u>I am Curious Yellow</u>. Local church groups and others offended by the film's graphic sex scenes, picketed the film. On June 6, 1969, the theater was the victim of arson. The theater was "probably burned in the name of decency by some misguided moralists," quoted one newspaper interview. Others surmised the fire was set by unionized film operators who protested the theater's non-union status. From 1969 until 1981, Heights Theater became a "ghost cinema," with only its shell remaining and an "open-air" roof. In 1981, Jim Holland purchased and began renovation the building. It changed hands again in 1988 to its present owners, Gus and Sharon Kopriva, who completed renovation of the building in 1990. Today, it is the location for art exhibits, theater productions, benefits and parties. (Photograph courtesy of Houston Public Library, HMRC)

Two photographs, taken 30 years apart, depict the decline experienced by the entire Heights community as a residential neighborhood and business district. Pictured here is 19th Avenue, which had always remained the central business district and hub of activity for the neighborhood, until it began to experience decline in the 1940s. Newly constructed highway systems led young families to new "suburban" living coupled with the explosive growth of Houston, put increased strain on the city. Older neighborhoods, as a result, were ignored and a slow decline came to the area. As founders passed, their homes were razed or converted into rental property and the perception of the Heights by 1970, was that of poverty. Little was heard about the Heights however, until August 1973, when one of the nation's biggest horror stories became associated with the community. Elmer Wayne Henley, a convicted murderer, and many of his victims were from the Heights. After this story made headlines, a group of community and business leaders decided to take action, forming the Houston Heights Association in an effort to put a halt to any further decline. Since that time, the community's revitalization, (now almost 20 years in the works) has received national, as well as city and state recognition. (Photographs courtesy of Houston Public Library, HMRC and Parsley Studios)

This Greek Revival house, originally located at 1002 Harvard Street, was constructed as the rectory for All Saints Catholic Church in 1912. In 1927, the old church was demolished, a new church was built and the Rectory was put up for sale to be moved. Patrick Francis Doyle purchased it and moved the house by lowering it onto logs, then pulling the structure with mule teams to its present location at 943 1/2 Cortlandt Street. It took two days to move the house from 10th and Harvard Streets to the present site only two blocks away. The house was used as a boarding house and then as rental property. From 1964 to 1987, the house remained vacant. It was purchased, renovated and sold to its present owners in 1988. This photograph of the house was taken by Houston photographer Geoff Winningham in 1985. (Photograph donated by Geoff Winningham to Heights Museum Collection)

G.W. Hawkins Day, celebrated on September 21, 1975, on Heights Boulevard, was the beginning of an annual event which is now known as the Heights Festival. This old-fashioned celebration was organized in honor of G.W. Hawkins, who first moved to Houston Heights in 1904 and lived at 1201 Heights Boulevard. Hawkins reportedly drove the first automobile down Heights Boulevard on September 16, 1905. The celebration brought thousands to the Heights to mingle in a nostalgic venture into yesteryear. Many stood in line to tour old homes, as antique cars paraded on Heights Boulevard, ethnic dancers performed in the esplanade, and vendors peddled barbecue and soft drinks in the streets. The event was organized by Heights residents not only to celebrate the 70th anniversary of G.W. Hawkins' historic drive, but also to bring a new level of awareness concerning the Heights to other parts of the city. Today, the Heights Festival, in its 16th year spans more than nine blocks on Heights Boulevard and brings an estimated 20,000 people into the neighborhood every year. (Photograph by Houston Post photographer Danny Connolly and courtesy of Houston Public Library, HMRC)

Glenn Dickerson and son, Zack, are shown crossing the "finish line" at the first annual 5K Heights Fun Run in 1986. Taking place on Heights Boulevard, the "Fun Run" course follows the neighborhood's most scenic, historic street, Heights Boulevard. Like the Heights Historical Home Tour and Heights Festival, the Fun Run has become an annual Heights event. It attracts runners, joggers and walkers from all over the city. (Photograph by Jennifer Kiger for The Leader Newspapers and courtesy of Glenn Dickerson)

Debbie Drouin is seen here working on Heights Beautification Day , September 29, 1988, organized by the Main Street Project Beautification Committee to spruce up some of Houston Heights' main thoroughfares. The Houston Heights Main Street project, in partnership between the Greater Heights Area Chamber of Commerce and the City of Houston, has coordinated the revitalization of the historically significant business district of Houston Heights. The program addresses redevelopment through organization, promotion, design and economic development. Since January 1988, there have been 37 new business startups and 40 building rehabilitations, for a total private sector reinvestment of $2.5 million. (Photograph by Tracy Vessels and donated by The Leader Newspapers)

Richard Herdell, Chairman of the Deed Restriction Project of the Houston Heights Association, is seen here notarizing a deed restriction document during the "Saturday Project" in August 1990 — a grassroots effort to implement block-by-block deed restrictions in the Heights area. This project is the first of its kind in the city of Houston and has been highly successful. Since 1973, the Houston Heights Association has been the driving force behind the neighborhood's revitalization. The Houston Heights Association addresses the scope of neighborhoods needs—from deed restrictions, community assistance and crime, to beautification, historic preservation and restoration. Its fundraisers, (Heights 5K Fun Run, Historic Home Tour and Heights Festival) raise more than $40,000 annually to fund community projects which work to enhance the quality of life in Houston Heights. (Photograph by Tracy Vessels and donated of by The Leader Newspapers.)

Taken on the eve of 1991, this photograph clearly shows the close proximity of Houston Heights to downtown Houston. Houston Heights, named for its contiguity to Houston and its altitude — 23 feet higher than the city proper, was developed and flourished as an independent municipality until 1918 when it was annexed by the City of Houston. Even though modern Houston has completely surrounded the old boundaries of the City of Houston Heights, it is apparent upon driving into the area that Houston Heights still retains its unique, small town identity. While the passage of time and the push for "progress" have tried to erode the picturesque and historic existence of Houston Heights, it can be seen, by this 19th century home, towering above the trees, that this community remains, even today, very distinctive and apart from the huge, modern skyscrapers seen in the distance. (Photograph courtesy of Barry Byrd)

HOUSTON HEIGHTS
1991

A Contemporary Perspective ...

Todd August; 1984, *Untitled*, 2 - 8 1/2" x 12", Silver Gelatin

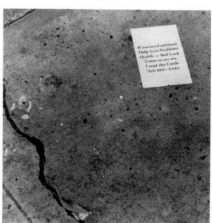

Gary Bankhead; 1990, *I Read The Cards*, 3 - 9" x 9", Silver Gelatin

Bruce Bennett; 1990, *Backyard Scene*, 13 1/2" x 9 1/8", Black & White

Dixon Bennett; 1990, *Boulevard Mist*, 9 1/2" x 13", Color

Suzanne Bloom; 1979, *White Oak Bayou Series*, 20" x 24", Color (courtesy of Moody Gallery)

"After more than 40 years, Stafford's last night in his apartment, Miss Mary's boarding house, 1237 Rutland."

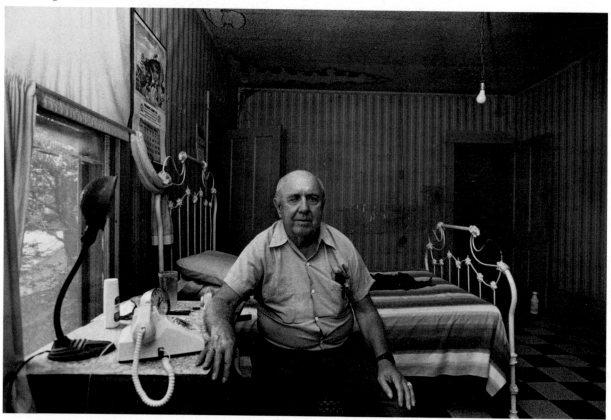

Donna Carson; 1989, *Forty Years of Memories*, 9" x 13 1/2", Silver Gelatin

"Theresa Brice teaches her daughter Lauren, 4, to ride
1100 block of Rutland."

Richard Carson; 1988, *Childhood Rite of Passage*, 13 1/2" x 9",
Color Negative to Panchromatic Silver Gelatin

George Craig; 1990, *Wet and Dry*, 2 - 12" x 12", Silver Gelatin

Jeff DeBevec; 1990, *A Clear Day in the Heights*, 14" x 22", Color Print

Robert Derr; 1991, *Welcome to the Heights*, 7 1/2" x 10 1/2", Black & White

Dave Einsel; 1990, *Untitled*, 12" x 9 3/4", Silver Gelatin

John Everett; 1990, *Washateria on Studewood*, 6" x 9", Black & White

Tom Fox; 1990, *White Oak Bayou Park*, 10 1/2" x 31", Color Print

Bill Frazier; 1990, *Houston, 1990*, 7 1/2" x 7 1/2", Silver Gelatin

Frank Golden; 1990, *Untitled*, 8" x 8", Black & White

Paul Hester; 1990, *Change 1990 @ 1441 Heights Blvd.*, 11" x 9 1/4",
Black & White, Color

Paul S. Howell; 1990, *Milroy House, Heights Boulevard*, 5" x 12", Black & White

C. Bryan Jones; 1987, *Opal's*, 8" x 8", Black & White

George Krause; 1985, *Skateboarder*, 4 1/2 x 6 1/2, Silver Gelatin Toned

Frank Martin; 1989, *Dark House*, 28" x 35", Black & White, retouched negative (private collection)

Please come to my house 742 East 16th street this Saturday from 10:00 o'clock A.M. until 1:00 or 1:30 P.M. for a neighborhood Christmas get together. Seems like neighbors should get together once a year. These garage sales give me a chance  to see all my neigh- bors. Oh, honey I love to paint, especially flowers. Come as you are, very informal, I will not have lots of Christmas goodies like I used to, age is telling on me. Sometimes I can barely remember the recipes. If you have children, bring them I love them. I'm looking forward to seeing you in my home on December 6th.

Essie Barnes, Mrs L L Barnes

I take Hope everywhere with me. I couldn't get along without Hope. She'll be sixteen if she lives to next June, but I don't think she'll make it. I've raised dogs all my life. I raised  two dogs to be 16! When we moved back here from Washington in 1956, my husband Mac put up this fence so that I could have a dog. He died on Thanks- giving day and my cousin Patsy brought me a Chihuahua named "Micky." I said "Oh Patsy, I don't want a dog," and she said "Yes you do, it'll do you good!" That Micky lived to be 16 years old. She died in that back bedroom. Now I've got Hope, and I don't know what I'd do without her. I love dogs.

Alice Ruth Thomas

Janice Rubin; 1990, *and my neighbor said...*, 2 - 10" x 8", Polaroid© Transfer Photograph

"Fireman Descending Staircase at Houston Heights Fire Station No. 14."

Tracy Vessels; 1987, *Untitled*, 11" x 14", Black & White

PHOTOGRAPHER BIOGRAPHIES

August, Todd; born 4-16-50 in New York, New York

Bankhead, Gary; born 6-24-53 in Houston, Texas

Bennett, Bruce; born 1-02-51 in Houston, Texas

Bennett, Dixon, born 9-18-43 in Austin, Texas

Bloom, Suzanne; born 1943 in Philadelphia, Pennsylvania

Carson, Donna; born 5-05-58 in Houston, Texas

Carson, Richard; born 3-15-56 in Lufkin, Texas

Craig, George; born 3-29-50 in Houston, Texas

DeBevec, Jeff; born 4-05-47 in Iron Mountain, Michigan

Derr, Robert; born 10-03-48 in Greeley, Colorado

Einsel, Dave; born 9-14-59 in Abilene, Texas

Everett, John; born 4-06-48 in Logan, West Virginia

Fox, Tom; born 6-15-46 in Cedar Rapids, Iowa

Frazier, Bill; born 8-16-52 in New Orleans, Louisiana

Golden, Frank; born 5-12-48 in Columbia, South Carolina

Hester, Paul; born 5-30-48 in Nashville, Tennessee

Howell, Paul S.; born 12-10-59 in Beaumont, Texas

Jones, C. Bryan; born 6-24-43 in Amarillo, Texas

Krause, George; born 1937 in Philadelphia, Pennsylvania

Martin, Frank; born 1942 in New Orleans, Louisiana

Rubin, Janice; born 8-20-55 in Fort Worth, Texas

Vessels, Tracy; born 5-25-64 in Amarillo, Texas

BIBLIOGRAPHY

Agatha, Sister M., <u>The History of Houston Heights 1891-1918</u>, Houston: Premier Printing Company, 1956

Carter, Mrs. Nellie, "Notes concerning Houston Heights," Typescript, 1928 (Sister M. Agatha Scrapbook Collection, Houston Metropolitan Research Library, Houston, Texas)

City Building in the New South: The Growth of Public Services in Houston, Texas, 1830-1910, Harold L. Platt, Philadelphia; Temple University Press

<u>City Directory of Boston, Massachusetts</u>

<u>City Directory of Houston, Texas and Houston Heights, Texas</u>

<u>City Directory of Lawrence, Massachusetts</u>

Dressman, Frances, "Visions for Houston: Booster Literature, 1886-1926," The Houston Review, Vol. IX, No. 3, Houston: Metropolitan Research Library, 1987

Green, Charles D., <u>Fire Fighters of Houston, 1838-1915</u>, Houston: no publisher, 1915

HEIGHTS CITIZEN, "Heights Golden Jubilee Edition"

HOUSTON CHRONICLE

HOUSTON DAILY HERALD, <u>Houston Illustrated, a Few Facts</u>, Houston: W.H. Coyle & Company, Printers, 1893

HOUSTON DAILY POST

Houston Heights Association (Lee Johnson and Peter Flagg Maxson, editors), National Register of Historic Places, Multiple Resource Area Nomination, April 1, 1981 (Approved June 28, 1983)

Houston Heights Charter, State of Texas House Bill No. 526, March 2, 1911, Houston Metropolitan Research Library, Houston, Texas

Houston Heights Realty Company, <u>Houston Heights, Houston's Oldest, Largest and Most Beautiful Suburb,</u> Houston: Omaha and South Texas Land Company, c. 1909

HOUSTON POST DISPATCH

HOUSTON PRESS "Houston Heights Golden Anniversary Issue" April 30, 1941

Incorporation Record, Omaha and South Texas Land Company, Book L, Page 59, Secretary of State, Austin, Texas, April 20, 1892

<u>The Industrial Advantages of Houston, Texas and Environs</u>, Houston: The Akehurst Publishing Company, 1894

Love, Mrs. W.G., editor, <u>The Key to the City of Houston</u>, "Suburbs of Houston," December 1908

Minutes, City Council, City of Houston Heights, Texas, City Secretary, City of Houston, Texas

Morse, Charles F., publisher, <u>The City of Houston, and Harris County, Texas, World's Columbian Exposition Souvenir</u>, Houston: Cumming & Sons, Printers, 1893

Pace, G. Randle, Application for Recorded Texas Historical Landmark for Houston Heights, Texas, typescript, 1990 (Approved 1991)

Real Property Records, County Clerk's office, Harris County, Texas

Sibley, Marilyn McAdams, <u>The Port of Houston, A History</u>, Austin: University of Texas Press, 1968

World Book Encyclopedia